THESE DREAMS BELONG TO:

BEDSIDE DREAM JOURNAL

A Nighttime Memory Book

CHRONICLE BOOKS
SAN FRANCISCO

ISBN 978-0-8118-7035-1

Manufactured in China.

Design by Grace Partridge.
Typeset in Bryant and Foxtrot.

Chronicle Books endeavors to use environmentally responsible paper in its gift and stationery products.

10 9 8 7 6 5 4 3 2 1

Chronicle Books LLC
680 Second Street
San Francisco, CA 94107
www.chroniclebooks.com

Introduction

HAVE YOU EVER WOKEN from a vivid and disorienting dream, utterly baffled and bemused? Let this dream journal guide you through the beguiling language of the unconscious and help you make sense of your dreams.

Record your dreams in this journal as soon as you wake, capturing as many details as you can remember. Call upon all your dream senses. The sounds, smells, emotions, and textures in your dreams can be just as telling as the events themselves. As the entries in your dream diary multiply, pick out striking or frequently recurring symbols or situations.

Next, search through the dream glossary, which features commentaries on key motifs and dream archetypes as diverse as mazes, money, and marriage. Locate the objects that relate to the images in your dream, keeping in mind that similar images or objects might hold the answers you seek (for example, the map description would still be relevant if the dream symbol you wanted to find out about were a compass, or a policeman giving directions, or a guiding star). Read the text, ask yourself the questions put to you, and reassess your dream or dreams in light of this newfound insight. Remember that the descriptions in the glossary do not give hard-and-fast answers. Instead, they guide you to your own conclusions based on the particularities of your dream life and of your waking life. Taken as a whole, they can be used as a phrase book to help you interpret the language of your unconscious and relate it to your current, waking circumstances.

The world of dreams can also be a therapeutic place—certain dreams have a profound effect on our outlook which can last for days or even weeks. Throughout this journal you will find information on guided visualizations of different scenarios that will help you germinate dreams for specific beneficial purposes, such as to trigger creative inspiration, relieve pent-up frustrations, or bolster self-esteem. Just before you go to sleep, meditate on these scenarios to plant the scene in your mind. Follow the stages step by step, gradually building up layers of detail. You may need several attempts before you are able to summon up a dream in this way, and to remember it when you wake, but it is well worth persevering.

Once you have mastered the art of interpreting your dreams, try expanding your dream menu by selecting a guided scenario, either singularly or in combination, to cue other types of dreams. Or take your dream cue from a scenario completely of your own invention. The only limit is your imagination, and, as you will discover through your dreams, your imagination is boundless.

date / /

DREAM DESCRIPTION ....

....

....

....

....

....

....

....

....

KEY SYMBOLS ....

....

INTERPRETATION NOTES

date / /

DREAM DESCRIPTION ....

....

....

....

....

....

....

....

....

....

KEY SYMBOLS ....

....

INTERPRETATION NOTES

date / /

DREAM DESCRIPTION

....

....

....

....

....

....

....

....

....

KEY SYMBOLS

....

INTERPRETATION NOTES

date / /

DREAM DESCRIPTION ....

....

....

....

....

....

....

....

....

....

KEY SYMBOLS ....

....

INTERPRETATION NOTES

date / /

DREAM DESCRIPTION ....

....

....

....

....

....

....

....

....

....

KEY SYMBOLS ....

....

INTERPRETATION NOTES

DREAM DESCRIPTION ....

....

....

....

....

....

....

....

....

....

KEY SYMBOLS ....

....

INTERPRETATION NOTES

date / /

DREAM DESCRIPTION

....

....

....

....

....

....

....

....

....

KEY SYMBOLS

....

....

INTERPRETATION NOTES

date / /

DREAM DESCRIPTION ....

....

....

....

....

....

....

....

....

....

KEY SYMBOLS ....

....

INTERPRETATION NOTES

date / /

DREAM DESCRIPTION

KEY SYMBOLS

INTERPRETATION NOTES

date / /

DREAM DESCRIPTION ....

....

....

....

....

....

....

....

....

....

KEY SYMBOLS ....

....

INTERPRETATION NOTES

DREAM DESCRIPTION ....

....

....

....

....

....

....

....

....

....

KEY SYMBOLS ....

....

INTERPRETATION NOTES

date   /   /

DREAM DESCRIPTION ....

....

....

....

....

....

....

....

....

....

KEY SYMBOLS ....

....

INTERPRETATION NOTES

DREAM DESCRIPTION

KEY SYMBOLS

INTERPRETATION NOTES

date   /   /

DREAM DESCRIPTION ....

....

....

....

....

....

....

....

....

KEY SYMBOLS ....

....

INTERPRETATION NOTES

date / /

DREAM DESCRIPTION

KEY SYMBOLS

INTERPRETATION NOTES

DREAM DESCRIPTION ....

....

....

....

....

....

....

....

....

....

KEY SYMBOLS ....

....

INTERPRETATION NOTES

date   /   /

DREAM DESCRIPTION

KEY SYMBOLS

INTERPRETATION NOTES

date / /

DREAM DESCRIPTION ....

....

....

....

....

....

....

....

....

....

KEY SYMBOLS ....

....

INTERPRETATION NOTES

date / /

DREAM DESCRIPTION

KEY SYMBOLS

INTERPRETATION NOTES

date / /

DREAM DESCRIPTION ....

....

....

....

....

....

....

....

....

....

KEY SYMBOLS ....

....

INTERPRETATION NOTES

DREAM DESCRIPTION

KEY SYMBOLS

INTERPRETATION NOTES

date / /

DREAM DESCRIPTION

KEY SYMBOLS

INTERPRETATION NOTES

date / /

DREAM DESCRIPTION ....

....

....

....

....

....

....

....

....

....

KEY SYMBOLS ....

....

INTERPRETATION NOTES

date / /

DREAM DESCRIPTION ....

....

....

....

....

....

....

....

....

....

KEY SYMBOLS ....

....

INTERPRETATION NOTES

date / /

DREAM DESCRIPTION

KEY SYMBOLS

INTERPRETATION NOTES

date / /

DREAM DESCRIPTION ....

....

....

....

....

....

....

....

....

KEY SYMBOLS ....

....

INTERPRETATION NOTES

date   /   /

DREAM DESCRIPTION ....

....

....

....

....

....

....

....

....

....

KEY SYMBOLS ....

....

INTERPRETATION NOTES

date / /

DREAM DESCRIPTION ....

....

....

....

....

....

....

....

....

KEY SYMBOLS ....

....

INTERPRETATION NOTES

date / /

DREAM DESCRIPTION ....

....

....

....

....

....

....

....

....

KEY SYMBOLS ....

....

INTERPRETATION NOTES

date / /

DREAM DESCRIPTION ....

....

....

....

....

....

....

....

....

....

KEY SYMBOLS ....

....

INTERPRETATION NOTES

date / /

DREAM DESCRIPTION

KEY SYMBOLS

INTERPRETATION NOTES

date / /

DREAM DESCRIPTION ....

....

....

....

....

....

....

....

....

KEY SYMBOLS ....

....

INTERPRETATION NOTES

date / /

DREAM DESCRIPTION ....

....

....

....

....

....

....

....

....

....

KEY SYMBOLS ....

....

INTERPRETATION NOTES

date   /   /

DREAM DESCRIPTION ....

....

....

....

....

....

....

....

....

....

KEY SYMBOLS ....

....

INTERPRETATION NOTES

DREAM DESCRIPTION

KEY SYMBOLS

INTERPRETATION NOTES

date   /   /

DREAM DESCRIPTION ....

....

....

....

....

....

....

....

....

KEY SYMBOLS ....

....

INTERPRETATION NOTES

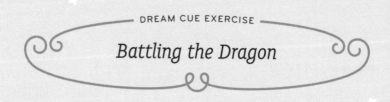

Battling the Dragon

OUR DREAM WORLD IS THE perfect place to build our self-esteem. By cuing dreams that see us overcome a dream adversary, we can gain confidence in our waking lives. Before you go to sleep, meditate on yourself as a dream hero. Imagine yourself in hero's finery, carrying a magical sword to defeat any foe. Visualize your obstacle as a dream dragon with all of your anxieties locked within its fiery jaws. Now visualize yourself brandishing your sword, and, with each swipe, the dragon retreats. Hold this image in your mind as you drift into sleep. The aim is to finally defeat the dragon in your dream.

DREAM DESCRIPTION

date / /

THOUGHTS OR FEELINGS ABOUT THIS DREAM

date   /   /

DREAM DESCRIPTION

KEY SYMBOLS

INTERPRETATION NOTES

date   /   /

DREAM DESCRIPTION ....

....

....

....

....

....

....

....

....

KEY SYMBOLS ....

....

INTERPRETATION NOTES

date / /

DREAM DESCRIPTION

....

....

....

....

....

....

....

....

....

....

KEY SYMBOLS

....

INTERPRETATION NOTES

date / /

DREAM DESCRIPTION ....

....

....

....

....

....

....

....

....

KEY SYMBOLS ....

....

INTERPRETATION NOTES

date / /

DREAM DESCRIPTION

KEY SYMBOLS

INTERPRETATION NOTES

date   /   /

DREAM DESCRIPTION ....

....

....

....

....

....

....

....

....

KEY SYMBOLS ....

....

INTERPRETATION NOTES

date / /

DREAM DESCRIPTION ....

....

....

....

....

....

....

....

....

....

KEY SYMBOLS ....

....

INTERPRETATION NOTES

date / /

DREAM DESCRIPTION ....

....

....

....

....

....

....

....

....

....

KEY SYMBOLS ....

....

INTERPRETATION NOTES

date / /

DREAM DESCRIPTION

_____

_____

_____

_____

_____

_____

_____

_____

_____

KEY SYMBOLS

_____

INTERPRETATION NOTES

date / /

DREAM DESCRIPTION ....

....

....

....

....

....

....

....

....

....

KEY SYMBOLS ....

....

INTERPRETATION NOTES

date / /

DREAM DESCRIPTION ....

....

....

....

....

....

....

....

....

....

KEY SYMBOLS ....

....

INTERPRETATION NOTES

date / /

DREAM DESCRIPTION ....

....

....

....

....

....

....

....

....

KEY SYMBOLS ....

....

INTERPRETATION NOTES

date / /

DREAM DESCRIPTION

KEY SYMBOLS

INTERPRETATION NOTES

date   /   /

DREAM DESCRIPTION

....

....

....

....

....

....

....

....

....

KEY SYMBOLS

....

INTERPRETATION NOTES

date / /

DREAM DESCRIPTION ....

....

....

....

....

....

....

....

....

....

KEY SYMBOLS ....

....

INTERPRETATION NOTES

date / /

DREAM DESCRIPTION ....

....

....

....

....

....

....

....

....

....

KEY SYMBOLS ....

....

INTERPRETATION NOTES

date   /   /

DREAM DESCRIPTION ....

....

....

....

....

....

....

....

....

....

KEY SYMBOLS ....

....

INTERPRETATION NOTES

date / /

DREAM DESCRIPTION ....

....

....

....

....

....

....

....

....

....

KEY SYMBOLS ....

....

INTERPRETATION NOTES

date / /

DREAM DESCRIPTION ....

....

....

....

....

....

....

....

....

....

KEY SYMBOLS ....

....

INTERPRETATION NOTES

date / /

DREAM DESCRIPTION ....

....

....

....

....

....

....

....

....

....

KEY SYMBOLS ....

....

INTERPRETATION NOTES

DREAM DESCRIPTION

KEY SYMBOLS

INTERPRETATION NOTES

date / /

DREAM DESCRIPTION ....

....

....

....

....

....

....

....

....

....

KEY SYMBOLS ....

....

INTERPRETATION NOTES

date   /   /

DREAM DESCRIPTION

KEY SYMBOLS

INTERPRETATION NOTES

date / /

DREAM DESCRIPTION

....

....

....

....

....

....

....

....

....

....

KEY SYMBOLS

....

INTERPRETATION NOTES

DREAM DESCRIPTION

KEY SYMBOLS

INTERPRETATION NOTES

date   /   /

DREAM DESCRIPTION ....

....

....

....

....

....

....

....

....

....

KEY SYMBOLS ....

....

INTERPRETATION NOTES

date   /   /

DREAM DESCRIPTION

KEY SYMBOLS

INTERPRETATION NOTES

DREAM DESCRIPTION ....

....

....

....

....

....

....

....

....

KEY SYMBOLS ....

....

INTERPRETATION NOTES

DREAM DESCRIPTION ....

....

....

....

....

....

....

....

....

KEY SYMBOLS ....

....

INTERPRETATION NOTES

date   /   /

DREAM DESCRIPTION ....

....

....

....

....

....

....

....

....

....

KEY SYMBOLS ....

....

INTERPRETATION NOTES

date / /

DREAM DESCRIPTION ....

....

....

....

....

....

....

....

....

KEY SYMBOLS ....

....

INTERPRETATION NOTES

date / /

DREAM DESCRIPTION ....

....

....

....

....

....

....

....

....

....

KEY SYMBOLS ....

....

INTERPRETATION NOTES

date / /

DREAM DESCRIPTION ....

....

....

....

....

....

....

....

....

....

KEY SYMBOLS ....

....

INTERPRETATION NOTES

date / /

DREAM DESCRIPTION ....

....

....

....

....

....

....

....

....

....

KEY SYMBOLS ....

....

INTERPRETATION NOTES

date / /

DREAM DESCRIPTION ....

....

....

....

....

....

....

....

....

....

KEY SYMBOLS ....

....

INTERPRETATION NOTES

date / /

DREAM DESCRIPTION ....

....

....

....

....

....

....

....

....

....

KEY SYMBOLS ....

....

INTERPRETATION NOTES

The Healing Place

AFTER AN ILLNESS, you may return to the normalcy of daily life while still feeling a little unwell. To help you develop a restorative frame of mind to complete your recovery, try to visualize a special healing place before you go to sleep. Perhaps this is a place that you always associate with healthy, happy days of childhood, such as a grandparent's garden. Alternatively, visualize an imagined calming place, such as a warm log cabin surrounded by snowcapped mountain peaks and the cleanest, freshest air. Hold the image of your recuperation in your mind as you drift into sleep. Visit it in your dreams and gain strength from its curative powers.

DREAM DESCRIPTION

date   /   /

THOUGHTS OR FEELINGS ABOUT THIS DREAM

date / /

DREAM DESCRIPTION ....

....

....

....

....

....

....

....

....

....

KEY SYMBOLS ....

....

INTERPRETATION NOTES

date / /

DREAM DESCRIPTION ....

....

....

....

....

....

....

....

....

....

KEY SYMBOLS ....

....

INTERPRETATION NOTES

date   /   /

DREAM DESCRIPTION ....

....

....

....

....

....

....

....

....

....

KEY SYMBOLS ....

....

INTERPRETATION NOTES

date / /

DREAM DESCRIPTION ....

....

....

....

....

....

....

....

....

....

KEY SYMBOLS ....

....

INTERPRETATION NOTES

DREAM DESCRIPTION

....

....

....

....

....

....

....

....

....

KEY SYMBOLS

....

INTERPRETATION NOTES

date   /   /

DREAM DESCRIPTION

KEY SYMBOLS

INTERPRETATION NOTES

date / /

DREAM DESCRIPTION ....

....

....

....

....

....

....

....

....

KEY SYMBOLS ....

....

INTERPRETATION NOTES

date / /

DREAM DESCRIPTION ....

....

....

....

....

....

....

....

....

....

KEY SYMBOLS ....

....

INTERPRETATION NOTES

date   /   /

DREAM DESCRIPTION

KEY SYMBOLS

INTERPRETATION NOTES

date / /

DREAM DESCRIPTION ....

....

....

....

....

....

....

....

....

....

KEY SYMBOLS ....

....

INTERPRETATION NOTES

DREAM DESCRIPTION

KEY SYMBOLS

INTERPRETATION NOTES

date   /   /

DREAM DESCRIPTION ....

....

....

....

....

....

....

....

....

....

KEY SYMBOLS ....

....

INTERPRETATION NOTES

DREAM DESCRIPTION ....

....

....

....

....

....

....

....

....

....

KEY SYMBOLS ....

....

INTERPRETATION NOTES

date   /   /

DREAM DESCRIPTION ....

....

....

....

....

....

....

....

....

KEY SYMBOLS ....

....

INTERPRETATION NOTES

date / /

DREAM DESCRIPTION ....

....

....

....

....

....

....

....

....

....

KEY SYMBOLS ....

....

INTERPRETATION NOTES

DREAM DESCRIPTION

KEY SYMBOLS

INTERPRETATION NOTES

date / /

DREAM DESCRIPTION ....

....

....

....

....

....

....

....

....

....

KEY SYMBOLS ....

....

INTERPRETATION NOTES

date / /

DREAM DESCRIPTION ....

....

....

....

....

....

....

....

....

....

KEY SYMBOLS ....

....

INTERPRETATION NOTES

date / /

DREAM DESCRIPTION ....

....

....

....

....

....

....

....

....

....

KEY SYMBOLS ....

....

INTERPRETATION NOTES

date / /

DREAM DESCRIPTION ....

....

....

....

....

....

....

....

....

....

KEY SYMBOLS ....

....

INTERPRETATION NOTES

date / /

DREAM DESCRIPTION ....

....

....

....

....

....

....

....

....

KEY SYMBOLS ....

....

INTERPRETATION NOTES

date / /

DREAM DESCRIPTION ....

....

....

....

....

....

....

....

....

....

KEY SYMBOLS ....

....

INTERPRETATION NOTES

date / /

DREAM DESCRIPTION

....

....

....

....

....

....

....

....

....

KEY SYMBOLS

....

INTERPRETATION NOTES

date / /

DREAM DESCRIPTION ....

....

....

....

....

....

....

....

....

....

KEY SYMBOLS ....

....

INTERPRETATION NOTES

DREAM DESCRIPTION

KEY SYMBOLS

INTERPRETATION NOTES

date / /

DREAM DESCRIPTION ....

....

....

....

....

....

....

....

....

....

KEY SYMBOLS ....

....

INTERPRETATION NOTES

date / /

DREAM DESCRIPTION

KEY SYMBOLS

INTERPRETATION NOTES

date / /

DREAM DESCRIPTION ....

....

....

....

....

....

....

....

....

....

KEY SYMBOLS ....

....

INTERPRETATION NOTES

date / /

DREAM DESCRIPTION ....

....

....

....

....

....

....

....

....

....

KEY SYMBOLS ....

....

INTERPRETATION NOTES

date   /   /

DREAM DESCRIPTION ....

....

....

....

....

....

....

....

....

....

KEY SYMBOLS ....

....

INTERPRETATION NOTES

DREAM DESCRIPTION

KEY SYMBOLS

INTERPRETATION NOTES

date   /   /

DREAM DESCRIPTION ....

....

....

....

....

....

....

....

....

....

KEY SYMBOLS ....

....

INTERPRETATION NOTES

date / /

DREAM DESCRIPTION ....

....

....

....

....

....

....

....

....

....

KEY SYMBOLS ....

....

INTERPRETATION NOTES

date   /   /

DREAM DESCRIPTION ....

....

....

....

....

....

....

....

....

....

KEY SYMBOLS ....

....

INTERPRETATION NOTES

date / /

DREAM DESCRIPTION

KEY SYMBOLS

INTERPRETATION NOTES

date   /   /

DREAM DESCRIPTION ....

....

....

....

....

....

....

....

....

....

KEY SYMBOLS ....

....

INTERPRETATION NOTES

date / /

DREAM DESCRIPTION ....

....

....

....

....

....

....

....

....

KEY SYMBOLS ....

....

INTERPRETATION NOTES

date　　　/　　　/

DREAM DESCRIPTION ....

....

....

....

....

....

....

....

....

....

KEY SYMBOLS ....

....

INTERPRETATION NOTES

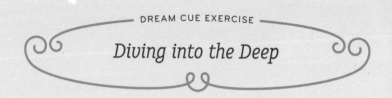

Diving into the Deep

BY USING CERTAIN CUES, we can encourage dreams that reveal hidden or buried aspects of ourselves. Before you sleep, imagine that you are lying on the seashore. Picture yourself swimming out into the ocean. The water is warm around you. Dive into the depths. You are perfectly safe and can breathe easily underwater. Imagine swimming into a wrecked ship, and exploring its many cabins. Fall asleep with the image of exploring the wreck in your mind, and feel confident that you will explore your unconscious in the same way. When you wake, what symbols from the unconscious did you rescue from your deep-sea dive?

DREAM DESCRIPTION

THOUGHTS OR FEELINGS ABOUT THIS DREAM

date / /

DREAM DESCRIPTION ....

....

....

....

....

....

....

....

....

....

KEY SYMBOLS ....

....

INTERPRETATION NOTES

date / /

DREAM DESCRIPTION

KEY SYMBOLS

INTERPRETATION NOTES

date / /

DREAM DESCRIPTION ....

....

....

....

....

....

....

....

....

....

....

KEY SYMBOLS ....

....

INTERPRETATION NOTES

date / /

DREAM DESCRIPTION ....

....

....

....

....

....

....

....

....

....

KEY SYMBOLS ....

....

INTERPRETATION NOTES

date / /

DREAM DESCRIPTION ....

....

....

....

....

....

....

....

....

....

KEY SYMBOLS ....

....

INTERPRETATION NOTES

date / /

DREAM DESCRIPTION ....

....

....

....

....

....

....

....

....

....

KEY SYMBOLS ....

....

INTERPRETATION NOTES

date / /

DREAM DESCRIPTION

KEY SYMBOLS

INTERPRETATION NOTES

date   /   /

DREAM DESCRIPTION ....

....

....

....

....

....

....

....

....

....

KEY SYMBOLS ....

....

INTERPRETATION NOTES

DREAM DESCRIPTION

KEY SYMBOLS

INTERPRETATION NOTES

date   /   /

DREAM DESCRIPTION ....

....

....

....

....

....

....

....

....

....

KEY SYMBOLS ....

....

INTERPRETATION NOTES

date / /

DREAM DESCRIPTION ....

....

....

....

....

....

....

....

....

KEY SYMBOLS ....

....

INTERPRETATION NOTES

date / /

DREAM DESCRIPTION ....

....

....

....

....

....

....

....

....

....

....

KEY SYMBOLS ....

....

INTERPRETATION NOTES

date / /

DREAM DESCRIPTION

....

....

....

....

....

....

....

....

....

KEY SYMBOLS

....

....

INTERPRETATION NOTES

date / /

DREAM DESCRIPTION ....

....

....

....

....

....

....

....

....

....

KEY SYMBOLS ....

....

INTERPRETATION NOTES

date   /   /

DREAM DESCRIPTION ....

....

....

....

....

....

....

....

....

KEY SYMBOLS ....

....

INTERPRETATION NOTES

date / /

DREAM DESCRIPTION ....

....

....

....

....

....

....

....

....

....

KEY SYMBOLS ....

....

INTERPRETATION NOTES

date   /   /

DREAM DESCRIPTION

KEY SYMBOLS

INTERPRETATION NOTES

date / /

DREAM DESCRIPTION ....

....

....

....

....

....

....

....

....

....

KEY SYMBOLS ....

....

INTERPRETATION NOTES

date / /

DREAM DESCRIPTION ....

....

....

....

....

....

....

....

....

....

KEY SYMBOLS ....

....

INTERPRETATION NOTES

date   /   /

DREAM DESCRIPTION ....

....

....

....

....

....

....

....

....

KEY SYMBOLS ....

....

INTERPRETATION NOTES

date / /

DREAM DESCRIPTION ....

....

....

....

....

....

....

....

....

KEY SYMBOLS ....

....

INTERPRETATION NOTES

DREAM DESCRIPTION

....

....

....

....

....

....

....

....

....

....

KEY SYMBOLS

....

INTERPRETATION NOTES

date / /

DREAM DESCRIPTION ....

....

....

....

....

....

....

....

....

....

KEY SYMBOLS ....

....

INTERPRETATION NOTES

date / /

DREAM DESCRIPTION

....

....

....

....

....

....

....

....

....

....

KEY SYMBOLS

....

INTERPRETATION NOTES

date / /

DREAM DESCRIPTION

....

....

....

....

....

....

....

....

....

KEY SYMBOLS

....

INTERPRETATION NOTES

date / /

DREAM DESCRIPTION ....

....

....

....

....

....

....

....

....

....

KEY SYMBOLS ....

....

INTERPRETATION NOTES

date   /   /

DREAM DESCRIPTION

KEY SYMBOLS

INTERPRETATION NOTES

date / /

DREAM DESCRIPTION ....

....

....

....

....

....

....

....

....

....

KEY SYMBOLS ....

....

INTERPRETATION NOTES

date / /

DREAM DESCRIPTION

KEY SYMBOLS

INTERPRETATION NOTES

date / /

DREAM DESCRIPTION

....

....

....

....

....

....

....

....

....

....

KEY SYMBOLS

....

INTERPRETATION NOTES

date / /

DREAM DESCRIPTION

....

....

....

....

....

....

....

....

....

KEY SYMBOLS

....

INTERPRETATION NOTES

date   /   /

DREAM DESCRIPTION

KEY SYMBOLS

INTERPRETATION NOTES

date / /

DREAM DESCRIPTION ....

....

....

....

....

....

....

....

....

....

KEY SYMBOLS ....

....

INTERPRETATION NOTES

date / /

DREAM DESCRIPTION ....

....

....

....

....

....

....

....

....

KEY SYMBOLS ....

....

INTERPRETATION NOTES

date / /

DREAM DESCRIPTION

KEY SYMBOLS

INTERPRETATION NOTES

date / /

DREAM DESCRIPTION ....

....

....

....

....

....

....

....

....

....

KEY SYMBOLS ....

....

INTERPRETATION NOTES

Revealing Hidden Love

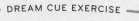

IF YOU HOLD FEELINGS FOR SOMEONE, but are unsure about how to approach the object of your affection, ask your dreams for help. Hold the image of your loved one in your mind as you drift into sleep. When you wake in the morning, search your dreams for signs of the person. They may not have appeared in literal, physical form, but symbolically. For example, think about what color you associate with the person. Did this color appear in your dream? How did your dream-self feel when encountering symbols of your love—warm or cold, brave or fearful, happy or sad? What might your dreams be trying to tell you about revealing your feelings to your love?

DREAM DESCRIPTION

THOUGHTS OR FEELINGS ABOUT THIS DREAM

date   /   /

DREAM DESCRIPTION ....

....

....

....

....

....

....

....

....

KEY SYMBOLS ....

....

INTERPRETATION NOTES

date / /

DREAM DESCRIPTION ....

....

....

....

....

....

....

....

....

....

KEY SYMBOLS ....

....

INTERPRETATION NOTES

date / /

DREAM DESCRIPTION

....

....

....

....

....

....

....

....

KEY SYMBOLS

....

INTERPRETATION NOTES

date / /

DREAM DESCRIPTION

KEY SYMBOLS

INTERPRETATION NOTES

date / /

DREAM DESCRIPTION

KEY SYMBOLS

INTERPRETATION NOTES

date   /   /

DREAM DESCRIPTION ....

....

....

....

....

....

....

....

....

....

KEY SYMBOLS ....

....

INTERPRETATION NOTES

date   /   /

DREAM DESCRIPTION ....

....

....

....

....

....

....

....

....

....

KEY SYMBOLS ....

....

INTERPRETATION NOTES

date　　/　　　/

DREAM DESCRIPTION

....

....

....

....

....

....

....

....

....

KEY SYMBOLS

....

INTERPRETATION NOTES

date / /

DREAM DESCRIPTION ....

....

....

....

....

....

....

....

....

....

KEY SYMBOLS ....

....

INTERPRETATION NOTES

date / /

DREAM DESCRIPTION ....

....

....

....

....

....

....

....

....

KEY SYMBOLS ....

....

INTERPRETATION NOTES

date / /

DREAM DESCRIPTION ....

....

....

....

....

....

....

....

....

....

KEY SYMBOLS ....

....

INTERPRETATION NOTES

date / /

DREAM DESCRIPTION ....

....

....

....

....

....

....

....

....

KEY SYMBOLS ....

....

INTERPRETATION NOTES

date / /

DREAM DESCRIPTION

....

....

....

....

....

....

....

....

....

....

KEY SYMBOLS

....

INTERPRETATION NOTES

date / /

DREAM DESCRIPTION

....

....

....

....

....

....

....

....

....

KEY SYMBOLS

....

INTERPRETATION NOTES

date / /

DREAM DESCRIPTION ....

....

....

....

....

....

....

....

....

....

KEY SYMBOLS ....

....

INTERPRETATION NOTES

date / /

DREAM DESCRIPTION

KEY SYMBOLS

INTERPRETATION NOTES

date / /

DREAM DESCRIPTION ....

....

....

....

....

....

....

....

....

....

KEY SYMBOLS ....

....

INTERPRETATION NOTES

date   /   /

DREAM DESCRIPTION ....

....

....

....

....

....

....

....

....

....

....

KEY SYMBOLS ....

....

INTERPRETATION NOTES

date / /

DREAM DESCRIPTION ....

....

....

....

....

....

....

....

....

....

KEY SYMBOLS ....

....

INTERPRETATION NOTES

date / /

DREAM DESCRIPTION ....

....

....

....

....

....

....

....

....

....

KEY SYMBOLS ....

....

INTERPRETATION NOTES

DREAM DESCRIPTION ....

....

....

....

....

....

....

....

....

....

KEY SYMBOLS ....

....

INTERPRETATION NOTES

date / /

DREAM DESCRIPTION ....

....

....

....

....

....

....

....

....

KEY SYMBOLS ....

....

INTERPRETATION NOTES

date   /   /

DREAM DESCRIPTION

KEY SYMBOLS

INTERPRETATION NOTES

date / /

DREAM DESCRIPTION

KEY SYMBOLS

INTERPRETATION NOTES

date   /   /

DREAM DESCRIPTION ....

....

....

....

....

....

....

....

....

....

KEY SYMBOLS ....

....

INTERPRETATION NOTES

date   /   /

DREAM DESCRIPTION ....

....

....

....

....

....

....

....

....

....

KEY SYMBOLS ....

....

INTERPRETATION NOTES

date / /

DREAM DESCRIPTION ....

....

....

....

....

....

....

....

....

....

KEY SYMBOLS ....

....

INTERPRETATION NOTES

date / /

DREAM DESCRIPTION ....

....

....

....

....

....

....

....

....

....

KEY SYMBOLS ....

....

INTERPRETATION NOTES

date   /   /

DREAM DESCRIPTION

....

....

....

....

....

....

....

....

....

KEY SYMBOLS

....

INTERPRETATION NOTES

date / /

DREAM DESCRIPTION ....

....

....

....

....

....

....

....

....

....

KEY SYMBOLS ....

....

INTERPRETATION NOTES

date   /   /

DREAM DESCRIPTION ....

....

....

....

....

....

....

....

....

....

KEY SYMBOLS ....

....

INTERPRETATION NOTES

date   /   /

DREAM DESCRIPTION ....

....

....

....

....

....

....

....

....

....

KEY SYMBOLS ....

....

INTERPRETATION NOTES

date　　/　　　/

DREAM DESCRIPTION ....

....

....

....

....

....

....

....

....

KEY SYMBOLS ....

....

INTERPRETATION NOTES

date / /

DREAM DESCRIPTION ....

....

....

....

....

....

....

....

....

....

KEY SYMBOLS ....

....

INTERPRETATION NOTES

date / /

DREAM DESCRIPTION

KEY SYMBOLS

INTERPRETATION NOTES

date / /

DREAM DESCRIPTION ....

....

....

....

....

....

....

....

....

....

KEY SYMBOLS ....

....

INTERPRETATION NOTES

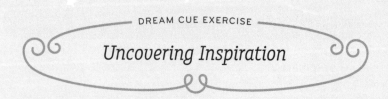

Uncovering Inspiration

AT CERTAIN POINTS IN OUR LIVES, we may find ourselves fumbling for inspiration. Certain methods of dreaming can help us unblock our creative channels. Try spending some time studying a reproduction of a painting that you find particularly intriguing or evocative. Imagine details that are outside the frame, or behind walls, or obscured by shadow. In the morning, see if you can remember any features from your dreams that you visualized in the painting. How did your subconscious treat the material that your conscious imagination provided?

DREAM DESCRIPTION

THOUGHTS OR FEELINGS ABOUT THIS DREAM

date   /   /

DREAM DESCRIPTION ....

....

....

....

....

....

....

....

....

KEY SYMBOLS ....

....

INTERPRETATION NOTES

date / /

DREAM DESCRIPTION

KEY SYMBOLS

INTERPRETATION NOTES

date   /   /

DREAM DESCRIPTION ....

....

....

....

....

....

....

....

....

....

KEY SYMBOLS ....

....

INTERPRETATION NOTES

date / /

DREAM DESCRIPTION ....

....

....

....

....

....

....

....

....

KEY SYMBOLS ....

....

INTERPRETATION NOTES

date   /   /

DREAM DESCRIPTION

KEY SYMBOLS

INTERPRETATION NOTES

date   /   /

DREAM DESCRIPTION ....

....

....

....

....

....

....

....

....

KEY SYMBOLS ....

....

INTERPRETATION NOTES

date   /   /

DREAM DESCRIPTION

KEY SYMBOLS

INTERPRETATION NOTES

date /   /

DREAM DESCRIPTION ....

....

....

....

....

....

....

....

....

....

KEY SYMBOLS ....

....

INTERPRETATION NOTES

DREAM DESCRIPTION

KEY SYMBOLS

INTERPRETATION NOTES

date / /

DREAM DESCRIPTION ....

....

....

....

....

....

....

....

....

....

KEY SYMBOLS ....

....

INTERPRETATION NOTES

date / /

DREAM DESCRIPTION ....

....

....

....

....

....

....

....

....

....

KEY SYMBOLS ....

....

INTERPRETATION NOTES

date   /   /

DREAM DESCRIPTION

KEY SYMBOLS

INTERPRETATION NOTES

DREAM DESCRIPTION

KEY SYMBOLS

INTERPRETATION NOTES

date   /   /

DREAM DESCRIPTION ....

....

....

....

....

....

....

....

....

....

KEY SYMBOLS ....

....

INTERPRETATION NOTES

date   /   /

DREAM DESCRIPTION

KEY SYMBOLS

INTERPRETATION NOTES

date / /

DREAM DESCRIPTION ....

....

....

....

....

....

....

....

....

....

KEY SYMBOLS ....

....

INTERPRETATION NOTES

date   /   /

DREAM DESCRIPTION

....

....

....

....

....

....

....

....

....

KEY SYMBOLS

....

INTERPRETATION NOTES

DREAM DESCRIPTION

....

....

....

....

....

....

....

....

....

KEY SYMBOLS

....

INTERPRETATION NOTES

date / /

DREAM DESCRIPTION ....

....

....

....

....

....

....

....

....

....

KEY SYMBOLS ....

....

INTERPRETATION NOTES

date / /

DREAM DESCRIPTION ....

....

....

....

....

....

....

....

....

....

KEY SYMBOLS ....

....

INTERPRETATION NOTES

date / /

DREAM DESCRIPTION ....

....

....

....

....

....

....

....

....

....

KEY SYMBOLS ....

....

INTERPRETATION NOTES

date / /

DREAM DESCRIPTION ....

....

....

....

....

....

....

....

....

....

KEY SYMBOLS ....

....

INTERPRETATION NOTES

date   /   /

DREAM DESCRIPTION ....

....

....

....

....

....

....

....

....

KEY SYMBOLS ....

....

INTERPRETATION NOTES

date / /

DREAM DESCRIPTION

....

....

....

....

....

....

....

....

....

....

KEY SYMBOLS ....

....

INTERPRETATION NOTES

date   /   /

DREAM DESCRIPTION ....

....

....

....

....

....

....

....

....

KEY SYMBOLS ....

....

INTERPRETATION NOTES

date   /   /

DREAM DESCRIPTION ....

....

....

....

....

....

....

....

....

KEY SYMBOLS ....

....

INTERPRETATION NOTES

date / /

DREAM DESCRIPTION ....

....

....

....

....

....

....

....

....

....

....

KEY SYMBOLS ....

....

INTERPRETATION NOTES

date / /

DREAM DESCRIPTION ....

....

....

....

....

....

....

....

....

....

KEY SYMBOLS ....

....

INTERPRETATION NOTES

DREAM DESCRIPTION ....

....

....

....

....

....

....

....

....

....

KEY SYMBOLS ....

....

INTERPRETATION NOTES

date   /   /

DREAM DESCRIPTION ....

....

....

....

....

....

....

....

....

....

KEY SYMBOLS ....

....

INTERPRETATION NOTES

date   /   /

DREAM DESCRIPTION ....

....

....

....

....

....

....

....

....

....

KEY SYMBOLS ....

....

INTERPRETATION NOTES

DREAM DESCRIPTION ....

....

....

....

....

....

....

....

....

....

KEY SYMBOLS ....

....

INTERPRETATION NOTES

DREAM DESCRIPTION ....

....

....

....

....

....

....

....

....

....

KEY SYMBOLS ....

....

INTERPRETATION NOTES

date / /

DREAM DESCRIPTION ....

....

....

....

....

....

....

....

....

....

KEY SYMBOLS ....

....

INTERPRETATION NOTES

date / /

DREAM DESCRIPTION

KEY SYMBOLS

INTERPRETATION NOTES

date / /

DREAM DESCRIPTION ....

....

....

....

....

....

....

....

....

....

KEY SYMBOLS ....

....

INTERPRETATION NOTES

date / /

DREAM DESCRIPTION

KEY SYMBOLS

INTERPRETATION NOTES

date / /

DREAM DESCRIPTION ....

....

....

....

....

....

....

....

....

....

....

KEY SYMBOLS ....

....

INTERPRETATION NOTES

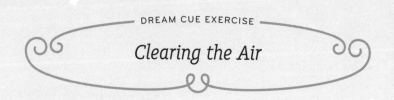

Clearing the Air

FEELINGS OF FRUSTRATION ARE a common by-product of modern life. Summoning up the power of the elements—air, water, earth, and fire—through visualization can encourage dreams that will help release pent-up irritation. Before sleep, imagine a landscape, sweltering beneath a sultry sky. A heavy rain begins to fall, hard enough to bounce off the rooftops. Forks of lightning sear through the clouds and a wild, bracing wind whips the earth. Suddenly the storm subsides, and the sun shines. Imagine breathing in the cool, fresh air. Drift into sleep with a thundercloud enveloping your mind, and prepare for it to burst in your dreams.

DREAM DESCRIPTION

THOUGHTS OR FEELINGS ABOUT THIS DREAM

date / /

DREAM DESCRIPTION

KEY SYMBOLS

INTERPRETATION NOTES

date / /

DREAM DESCRIPTION

KEY SYMBOLS

INTERPRETATION NOTES

date / /

DREAM DESCRIPTION ....

....

....

....

....

....

....

....

....

....

KEY SYMBOLS ....

....

INTERPRETATION NOTES

date / /

DREAM DESCRIPTION ....

....

....

....

....

....

....

....

....

....

KEY SYMBOLS ....

....

INTERPRETATION NOTES

date / /

DREAM DESCRIPTION ....

....

....

....

....

....

....

....

....

....

KEY SYMBOLS ....

....

INTERPRETATION NOTES

date   /   /

DREAM DESCRIPTION ....

....

....

....

....

....

....

....

....

KEY SYMBOLS ....

....

INTERPRETATION NOTES

date / /

DREAM DESCRIPTION

KEY SYMBOLS

INTERPRETATION NOTES

date / /

DREAM DESCRIPTION ....

....

....

....

....

....

....

....

....

....

KEY SYMBOLS ....

....

INTERPRETATION NOTES

date / /

DREAM DESCRIPTION

KEY SYMBOLS

INTERPRETATION NOTES

date / /

DREAM DESCRIPTION

....

....

....

....

....

....

....

....

....

....

KEY SYMBOLS

....

INTERPRETATION NOTES

date / /

DREAM DESCRIPTION ....

....

....

....

....

....

....

....

....

....

KEY SYMBOLS ....

....

INTERPRETATION NOTES

date / /

DREAM DESCRIPTION ....

....

....

....

....

....

....

....

....

....

KEY SYMBOLS ....

....

INTERPRETATION NOTES

date   /   ·   /

DREAM DESCRIPTION

KEY SYMBOLS

INTERPRETATION NOTES

date / /

DREAM DESCRIPTION ....

....

....

....

....

....

....

....

....

....

KEY SYMBOLS ....

....

INTERPRETATION NOTES

date / /

DREAM DESCRIPTION ....

....

....

....

....

....

....

....

....

KEY SYMBOLS ....

....

INTERPRETATION NOTES

date   /   /

DREAM DESCRIPTION ....

....

....

....

....

....

....

....

....

....

KEY SYMBOLS ....

....

INTERPRETATION NOTES

DREAM DESCRIPTION

KEY SYMBOLS

INTERPRETATION NOTES

date / /

DREAM DESCRIPTION ....

....

....

....

....

....

....

....

....

....

KEY SYMBOLS ....

....

INTERPRETATION NOTES

date / /

DREAM DESCRIPTION ....

....

....

....

....

....

....

....

....

KEY SYMBOLS ....

....

INTERPRETATION NOTES

date / /

DREAM DESCRIPTION

....

....

....

....

....

....

....

....

....

KEY SYMBOLS

....

INTERPRETATION NOTES

date   /   /

DREAM DESCRIPTION

KEY SYMBOLS

INTERPRETATION NOTES

date   /   /

DREAM DESCRIPTION

KEY SYMBOLS

INTERPRETATION NOTES

date / /

DREAM DESCRIPTION ....

....

....

....

....

....

....

....

....

....

KEY SYMBOLS ....

....

INTERPRETATION NOTES

date / /

DREAM DESCRIPTION

KEY SYMBOLS

INTERPRETATION NOTES

DREAM DESCRIPTION

KEY SYMBOLS

INTERPRETATION NOTES

date   /   /

DREAM DESCRIPTION ....

....

....

....

....

....

....

....

....

....

KEY SYMBOLS ....

....

INTERPRETATION NOTES

DREAM DESCRIPTION

KEY SYMBOLS

INTERPRETATION NOTES

date / /

DREAM DESCRIPTION ....

....

....

....

....

....

....

....

....

....

KEY SYMBOLS ....

....

INTERPRETATION NOTES

date   /   /

DREAM DESCRIPTION

KEY SYMBOLS

INTERPRETATION NOTES

date / /

DREAM DESCRIPTION ....

....

....

....

....

....

....

....

....

....

KEY SYMBOLS ....

....

INTERPRETATION NOTES

date / /

DREAM DESCRIPTION ....

....

....

....

....

....

....

....

....

....

KEY SYMBOLS ....

....

INTERPRETATION NOTES

date / /

DREAM DESCRIPTION ....

....

....

....

....

....

....

....

....

....

KEY SYMBOLS ....

....

INTERPRETATION NOTES

DREAM DESCRIPTION ....

....

....

....

....

....

....

....

....

KEY SYMBOLS ....

....

INTERPRETATION NOTES

date / /

DREAM DESCRIPTION ....

....

....

....

....

....

....

....

....

....

KEY SYMBOLS ....

....

INTERPRETATION NOTES

date   /   /

DREAM DESCRIPTION

KEY SYMBOLS

INTERPRETATION NOTES

date   /   /

DREAM DESCRIPTION ....

....

....

....

....

....

....

....

....

....

KEY SYMBOLS ....

....

INTERPRETATION NOTES

date / /

DREAM DESCRIPTION ....

....

....

....

....

....

....

....

....

....

KEY SYMBOLS ....

....

INTERPRETATION NOTES

date / /

DREAM DESCRIPTION ....

....

....

....

....

....

....

....

....

....

KEY SYMBOLS ....

....

INTERPRETATION NOTES

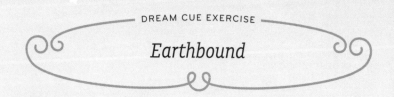

Earthbound

IN AN AGE DOMINATED BY TECHNOLOGY, it is easy to lose touch with the natural world. Dreams provide an ideal space to re-establish this vital connection. As you prepare for sleep, picture yourself alone on the moon. Feeling trapped inside a spacesuit, you gaze with longing at Earth, poised, fragile in a vast universe. Reaching out toward it, you find yourself hurtling through space, plunging naked into the swirling blue of the stratosphere. As you drift into sleep, luxuriate in the freedom of your body, awakening in the morning to a renewed sense of oneness with the world.

DREAM DESCRIPTION

THOUGHTS OR FEELINGS ABOUT THIS DREAM

date   /   /

DREAM DESCRIPTION

KEY SYMBOLS

INTERPRETATION NOTES

date / /

DREAM DESCRIPTION ....

....

....

....

....

....

....

....

....

....

KEY SYMBOLS ....

....

INTERPRETATION NOTES

date / /

DREAM DESCRIPTION ....

....

....

....

....

....

....

....

....

....

KEY SYMBOLS ....

....

INTERPRETATION NOTES

DREAM DESCRIPTION

....

....

....

....

....

....

....

....

....

KEY SYMBOLS

....

INTERPRETATION NOTES

date   /   /

DREAM DESCRIPTION ....

....

....

....

....

....

....

....

....

KEY SYMBOLS ....

....

INTERPRETATION NOTES

date / /

DREAM DESCRIPTION ....

....

....

....

....

....

....

....

....

KEY SYMBOLS ....

....

INTERPRETATION NOTES

date / /

DREAM DESCRIPTION ....

....

....

....

....

....

....

....

....

....

KEY SYMBOLS ....

....

INTERPRETATION NOTES

date / /

DREAM DESCRIPTION

....

....

....

....

....

....

....

....

....

....

KEY SYMBOLS

....

INTERPRETATION NOTES

DREAM DESCRIPTION

....

....

....

....

....

....

....

....

KEY SYMBOLS

....

INTERPRETATION NOTES

date / /

DREAM DESCRIPTION ....

....

....

....

....

....

....

....

....

....

KEY SYMBOLS ....

....

INTERPRETATION NOTES

date   /   /

DREAM DESCRIPTION

....

....

....

....

....

....

....

....

KEY SYMBOLS

....

INTERPRETATION NOTES

date / /

DREAM DESCRIPTION ....

....

....

....

....

....

....

....

....

....

KEY SYMBOLS ....

....

INTERPRETATION NOTES

date   /   /

DREAM DESCRIPTION

KEY SYMBOLS

INTERPRETATION NOTES

date   /   /

DREAM DESCRIPTION ....

....

....

....

....

....

....

....

....

....

KEY SYMBOLS ....

....

INTERPRETATION NOTES

DREAM DESCRIPTION

....

....

....

....

....

....

....

....

....

KEY SYMBOLS

....

INTERPRETATION NOTES

date   /   /

DREAM DESCRIPTION ....

....

....

....

....

....

....

....

....

KEY SYMBOLS ....

....

INTERPRETATION NOTES

DREAM DESCRIPTION

....

....

....

....

....

....

....

....

....

KEY SYMBOLS

....

INTERPRETATION NOTES

date   /   /

DREAM DESCRIPTION ....

....

....

....

....

....

....

....

....

....

KEY SYMBOLS ....

....

INTERPRETATION NOTES

date / /

DREAM DESCRIPTION ....

....

....

....

....

....

....

....

....

....

....

KEY SYMBOLS ....

....

INTERPRETATION NOTES

date   /   /

DREAM DESCRIPTION

....

....

....

....

....

....

....

....

....

KEY SYMBOLS

....

INTERPRETATION NOTES

date / /

DREAM DESCRIPTION ....

....

....

....

....

....

....

....

....

....

KEY SYMBOLS ....

....

INTERPRETATION NOTES

date / /

DREAM DESCRIPTION

KEY SYMBOLS

INTERPRETATION NOTES

DREAM DESCRIPTION

KEY SYMBOLS

INTERPRETATION NOTES

date / /

DREAM DESCRIPTION ....

....

....

....

....

....

....

....

....

....

KEY SYMBOLS ....

....

INTERPRETATION NOTES

date / /

DREAM DESCRIPTION

KEY SYMBOLS

INTERPRETATION NOTES

date   /   /

DREAM DESCRIPTION ....

....

....

....

....

....

....

....

....

....

KEY SYMBOLS ....

....

INTERPRETATION NOTES

date / /

DREAM DESCRIPTION

KEY SYMBOLS

INTERPRETATION NOTES

date   /   /

DREAM DESCRIPTION ....

....

....

....

....

....

....

....

....

....

KEY SYMBOLS ....

....

INTERPRETATION NOTES

date / /

DREAM DESCRIPTION ....

....

....

....

....

....

....

....

....

KEY SYMBOLS ....

....

INTERPRETATION NOTES

DREAM DESCRIPTION

KEY SYMBOLS

INTERPRETATION NOTES

DREAM DESCRIPTION

KEY SYMBOLS

INTERPRETATION NOTES

date   /   /

DREAM DESCRIPTION ....

....

....

....

....

....

....

....

....

....

KEY SYMBOLS ....

....

INTERPRETATION NOTES

date / /

DREAM DESCRIPTION

KEY SYMBOLS

INTERPRETATION NOTES

date / /

DREAM DESCRIPTION ....

....

....

....

....

....

....

....

....

....

KEY SYMBOLS ....

....

INTERPRETATION NOTES

date / /

DREAM DESCRIPTION

KEY SYMBOLS

INTERPRETATION NOTES

date   /   /

DREAM DESCRIPTION

KEY SYMBOLS

INTERPRETATION NOTES

date / /

DREAM DESCRIPTION ....

....

....

....

....

....

....

....

....

....

KEY SYMBOLS ....

....

INTERPRETATION NOTES

DREAM DESCRIPTION ....

....

....

....

....

....

....

....

....

....

KEY SYMBOLS ....

....

INTERPRETATION NOTES

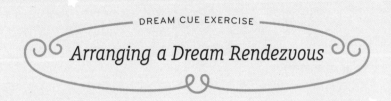

Arranging a Dream Rendezvous

SHARING A DREAM WITH SOMEONE you love is a powerful way to enhance the intimacy of your relationship. Before sleeping, choose, with your partner, a meeting place with pleasant emotional associations for you both. Visualize this place together, describing the details of each scene as you explore them in your mind. Arrange to meet at this location in your dreams, making the details as precise as possible and rehearsing them repeatedly in your mind. If you managed to coordinate successfully with your partner, compare your dreams carefully. Are there echoes between your dreams? What significance may these have for your relationship?

DREAM DESCRIPTION ....

....

....

....

....

....

....

....

THOUGHTS OR FEELINGS ABOUT THIS DREAM

date   /   /

DREAM DESCRIPTION

....

....

....

....

....

....

....

....

....

....

KEY SYMBOLS

....

INTERPRETATION NOTES

date / /

DREAM DESCRIPTION ....

....

....

....

....

....

....

....

....

....

KEY SYMBOLS ....

....

INTERPRETATION NOTES

date   /   /

DREAM DESCRIPTION ....

....

....

....

....

....

....

....

....

KEY SYMBOLS ....

....

INTERPRETATION NOTES

date   /   /

DREAM DESCRIPTION ....

....

....

....

....

....

....

....

....

KEY SYMBOLS ....

....

INTERPRETATION NOTES

date / /

DREAM DESCRIPTION ....

....

....

....

....

....

....

....

....

KEY SYMBOLS ....

....

INTERPRETATION NOTES

date   /   /

DREAM DESCRIPTION

....

....

....

....

....

....

....

....

....

KEY SYMBOLS

....

INTERPRETATION NOTES

date   /   /

DREAM DESCRIPTION

....

....

....

....

....

....

....

....

....

KEY SYMBOLS

....

INTERPRETATION NOTES

date / /

DREAM DESCRIPTION ....

....

....

....

....

....

....

....

....

....

KEY SYMBOLS ....

....

INTERPRETATION NOTES

DREAM DESCRIPTION ....

....

....

....

....

....

....

....

....

....

KEY SYMBOLS ....

....

INTERPRETATION NOTES

date / /

DREAM DESCRIPTION

....

....

....

....

....

....

....

....

....

....

KEY SYMBOLS

....

....

INTERPRETATION NOTES

date   /   /

DREAM DESCRIPTION ....

....

....

....

....

....

....

....

....

....

KEY SYMBOLS ....

....

INTERPRETATION NOTES

date   /   /

DREAM DESCRIPTION

KEY SYMBOLS

INTERPRETATION NOTES

DREAM DESCRIPTION ....

....

....

....

....

....

....

....

....

KEY SYMBOLS ....

....

INTERPRETATION NOTES

date / /

DREAM DESCRIPTION ....

....

....

....

....

....

....

....

....

KEY SYMBOLS ....

....

INTERPRETATION NOTES

date   /   /

DREAM DESCRIPTION

KEY SYMBOLS

INTERPRETATION NOTES

date   /   /

DREAM DESCRIPTION

KEY SYMBOLS

INTERPRETATION NOTES

date   /   /

DREAM DESCRIPTION

KEY SYMBOLS

INTERPRETATION NOTES

date / /

DREAM DESCRIPTION ....

....

....

....

....

....

....

....

....

....

KEY SYMBOLS ....

....

INTERPRETATION NOTES

date / /

DREAM DESCRIPTION

....

....

....

....

....

....

....

....

....

KEY SYMBOLS

....

....

INTERPRETATION NOTES

date   /   /

DREAM DESCRIPTION

....

....

....

....

....

....

....

....

....

KEY SYMBOLS

....

INTERPRETATION NOTES

date   /   /

DREAM DESCRIPTION ....

....

....

....

....

....

....

....

....

....

KEY SYMBOLS ....

....

INTERPRETATION NOTES

date / /

DREAM DESCRIPTION ....

....

....

....

....

....

....

....

....

....

KEY SYMBOLS ....

....

INTERPRETATION NOTES

DREAM DESCRIPTION

KEY SYMBOLS

INTERPRETATION NOTES

DREAM DESCRIPTION ....

....

....

....

....

....

....

....

....

KEY SYMBOLS ....

....

INTERPRETATION NOTES

date / /

DREAM DESCRIPTION ....

....

....

....

....

....

....

....

....

....

KEY SYMBOLS ....

....

INTERPRETATION NOTES

date   /   /

DREAM DESCRIPTION ....

....

....

....

....

....

....

....

....

....

KEY SYMBOLS ....

....

INTERPRETATION NOTES

date   /   /

DREAM DESCRIPTION ....

....

....

....

....

....

....

....

....

....

KEY SYMBOLS ....

....

INTERPRETATION NOTES

date / /

DREAM DESCRIPTION

KEY SYMBOLS

INTERPRETATION NOTES

date / /

DREAM DESCRIPTION

KEY SYMBOLS

INTERPRETATION NOTES

date / /

DREAM DESCRIPTION ....

....

....

....

....

....

....

....

....

....

....

KEY SYMBOLS ....

....

INTERPRETATION NOTES

date   /   /

DREAM DESCRIPTION ....

....

....

....

....

....

....

....

....

....

....

KEY SYMBOLS ....

....

INTERPRETATION NOTES

date   /   /

DREAM DESCRIPTION

KEY SYMBOLS

INTERPRETATION NOTES

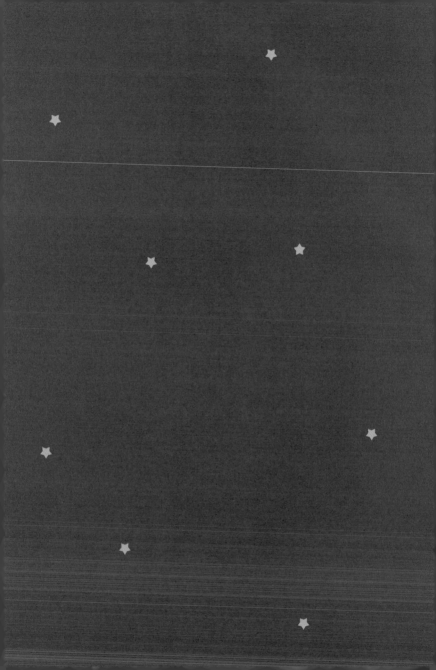

Dream Glossary

ABANDONMENT

The mind sometimes uses dreams as a form of therapy, enabling us to come to terms with painful experiences by reliving them through our subconscious. Dreaming of being abandoned may be an expression of feelings of loss or disappointment. Have you recently suffered bereavement, come to the end of a friendship, or split up with your partner? Has somebody close to you let you down? If your dream-self was still alone when the dream ended, search the dream landscape for signs of life. Were there lights in a distant house, or footprints in the road?

BEING CHASED

Dreams of being chased by an unseen but terrifying presence usually indicate that neglected aspects of the self are clamoring for our conscious attention. In Freudian psychoanalysis, confrontation rather than evasion is the strategy for coping with the "return of the repressed." Likewise in dreams, the fear of pursuit will often lessen if the dream-self can turn and face the chaser. Were you able to identify who or what was hounding you? What might this represent at a conscious level?

THE BELL

Images or the sound of bells often represent a message from the unconscious, perhaps a warning that unresolved issues now threaten to trouble the surface of the conscious mind. Are there conflicts or emotional wounds that you have brushed aside in waking life? Have you repressed any uncomfortable emotions? How did the bell appear in your dream? And how did your dream-self react to its chimes—with shock, with recognition, with dread?

BLINDNESS

If you dream that you cannot see, your unconscious may be hinting at a lack of self-awareness in your waking life. Can you identify the cause of your blindness? A blindfold or a refusal to open the eyes might suggest a failure to acknowledge problems in the external world. Alternatively, the blindness could signify internal conflicts that you are choosing to evade, or a sense of being lost, spiritually or emotionally, on life's path. Open your eyes. Use the symbols from your unconscious as guides to help you in the future.

THE BRIDGE

At certain points we face a dilemma over whether to make a crucial change. Is it time to look for another job, to move, or to bring an end to an unfulfilling relationship? Dreams in which we encounter a bridge provide our subconscious with an opportunity to act out the decision we have to make in our waking life. What sort of bridge did you come to in your dream? Was it sturdy and reliable, or was it made of rope and swaying in the wind? Did your dream-self decide to cross to the other side, or to turn back?

THE BULL
In some cases, the deeper significance of dream symbols is not immediately apparent. However, bulls in dreams carry the traditional connotations of sexuality and stubbornness. How did the bull in your dream act? Was it calmly grazing, asleep in its shed, butting against an immovable object, or charging through narrow cobbled streets? Can you draw any parallels between the bull's behavior and the current tempo of your sexual relationships? Or might it relate to an important matter over which you and someone else are locking horns?

THE CASTLE
Castles are built to keep invaders out and may convey positive images of security and protection. However, there is a danger that the very strength of our fortifications may be isolating us from others. Walk the ramparts of your dream castle once more. Did you see feasting and merriment in the banqueting hall? Were there embassies from neighboring kingdoms? Or were you huddled with your ministers in a council of war, preparing to be besieged?

CLIMBING
We might expect climbing dreams to indicate success and falling dreams failure, but other interpretations could reach a deeper level

of meaning. For Freud, climbing dreams represented a longing for sexual fulfillment, but they can also reflect aspirations in other areas of life, such as personal or professional growth. How easy or difficult did you find your dream climb? Did you encounter obstacles you could not overcome? If so, should you reassess your current goals and the ways in which you are trying to achieve them?

THE CLOCK

We sometimes refer to our heart colloquially as our "ticker," and so it follows that timepieces, when they appear in dreams, often stand for the emotional aspect of the dreamer's life. Close your eyes and re-create the clock or watch from your dream. Was it well-maintained, or chipped, scratched, and rusty? Did it keep the right time? Was its ticking regular, or did it race out of control in fits and starts? Did it not tick at all? Think of ways in which your dream timepiece may relate to your current emotional state.

CLOTHES

An ambivalent dream symbol, clothing is open to many possible interpretations, depending on the context of the dream and the circumstances of the dreamer. For example, a cloak may represent concealment, subterfuge, and mystery, or it might convey an enveloping sense of warmth, love, and protection. The line between positive and negative readings can be thin and indistinct, so try not to jump to conclusions that lead to undue unhappiness.

THE CROWN

The crown is a symbol of superiority and authority. Sometimes accompanied by a scepter, it can signify domination and is often linked with a sense of divine order. Did you identify with the crown in your dream? Who was wearing it—you, someone familiar to you, or a stranger? How did it appear? Was it burnished and encrusted with jewels, or tarnished through neglect? Consider how your dream crown might relate to your relationships with figures of authority.

DEATH

The collective unconscious takes the long-term view on death, associating it with change rather than with finality. Dreaming of death is often an expression of deep-seated anxieties within the dreamer. Are you approaching a period of transition that is worrying you—perhaps retirement, a career change, or a move? In your dream, were you the person who died, or was it someone else? Was there a funeral, a tombstone, or an obituary? What were your dream-self's feelings—relief, despair, or terror?

THE DIVINE CHILD

One of the most powerful archetypal symbols, the Divine Child represents perfection, rebirth, and the innocence of primal wisdom. Usually appearing in dreams as a baby or infant, it possesses tremendous transformative power, revealing the path to the true self. The presence of the Divine Child in a dream may be a reminder of your innate spiritual potential that has become obscured by material concerns. Pay attention to the child's words and deeds. Its advice could guide you to greater spiritual fulfillment in the future.

THE DOG

Often described as "man's best friend," a dog represents the loyalty typified in Greek mythology by Argos, the first creature to recognize Odysseus when he returned from his wanderings. The appearance of a dog in a dream can suggest a need for protection or platonic love. Did you communicate with the dog? What was the dog doing? Was it fierce or friendly, wild or tame? Consider how the behavior of the dog and your reactions to it might relate to your current friendships.

THE EGG

Used universally as a symbol in myth and art, the egg represents love, newness, birth, and opportunity. Always a positive sign, the dream egg stands for a fresh start. What new paths are you thinking about taking in waking life? Is there a job that you are considering? Are you thinking of starting a family or moving somewhere new? Could the egg be urging you to follow your heart, or is it expressing your anxieties about new ventures? How did it appear in your dream? How did your dream-self respond to its presence?

FALLING

One of the most common anxiety states while dreaming, a fall might represent fear of failure or a sense of tumbling into the unknown. Perhaps you have been thrust into something too quickly and are not yet secure in your position. Remember that, as with all aspects of our dream life, even in troubled or anxious dreams, we are making positive steps toward greater self-understanding. Take heed of the message of your dream falling. Treat your waking-self gently and remember that you deserve all your successes.

THE FISH

On the one hand, fish have commonly been used to symbolize divinity and the spiritual abundance that feeds us from the heavens. They can also, however, stand for what lies below the surface, in our subconscious. If the fish in your dream were caught in a net and hauled out of the water, they may represent unconscious insights brought into the full light of consciousness. Or did the fish slip through the mesh, off the hook, through your hands? Were they trapped in a tank, butting against glass walls? How can you use your dream to access the wisdom in your subconscious?

FLYING

The desire to rise into the air unaided is one of the central themes of human fantasy, embodied through the ages in characters from the winged god Mercury to the fictional hero Superman. Flying is one of the most exhilarating dream experiences, and the sense of elation that it brings can affect the dreamer's outlook for a long time after the dream. Embrace your flying dream. It is a reminder of your infinite spiritual and psychological potential. If you can fly, then nothing is out of your reach.

GIVING AND RECEIVING

Giving and receiving are symbolic forms of social interaction—
tokens of one person's esteem for another—and, as dream images,
may help us to assess our relationships with others. Scour your
dream for clues. Did you give the gift or receive it? Was the present
welcome or unwelcome, appropriate or inappropriate? Did it meet
expectations, or was the superficial wrapping more exciting than
the present itself? Did the recipient unwrap the package before you,
or did its contents remain a mystery?

THE HEART

In ancient Egyptian, Greek and Roman, and medieval European cul-
ture, parts of the body were used to denote aspects of the spiritual
world. The heart carries archetypal significance as the focus of emotional life, and especially as the symbol of love. In what form did
the heart in your dream appear? Were its beats fast and irregular, or
slow and calm? Could your subconscious be pointing out an unresolved issue affecting your relationship with your partner, or with a
member of your family?

HONEY

Honey has been prized since ancient times. The Greeks and Romans
regarded it as the food of the gods, and the Israelites associated the
abundance of the Promised Land with the milk and honey that they
believed flowed there. Appearing in a dream, honey is usually a positive, auspicious symbol. It may suggest prosperity or fertility. Are

you embarking on a new project—perhaps starting a business, or moving—and feeling in need of encouragement? Take heart from your honey dream!

THE HORSE

Horses in dreams often signify the instinctive energies and desires that we tend to tame, harness, or even suppress entirely, in our waking lives. How did the horse in your dream behave? Did it have a rider, or was it running wild? Did you appear in your dream? If so, how did your dream-self feel toward the horse—afraid? Awestruck? Contemptuous? Could your dream be urging you to slacken your grip on the reins, or might it be underlining the importance of self-control?

THE HOUSE

In dreams, a house often represents the dreamer, and the state of the house may reflect the dreamer's self-image or current circumstances. An empty or ruined house might signify a sense of loss. Have you recently suffered bereavement or the end of a close relationship? Or, on the other hand, was the house in your dream welcoming, warm, and comfortable—perhaps full of party guests? Were you inside, or were you outside, looking in? Take note of the state of your dream house, and what light that can shed on your current life.

THE INTERVIEW

Facing an interview panel for a job or an academic venture is one of the most stressful experiences most of us face in our waking lives, so it is little surprise that this scenario occurs frequently in our dreams. The interviewer or interviewers facing the dreamer may represent aspects of the self, suggesting a desire to hold oneself up to examination. Has anything happened to you recently in your waking life that could have prompted you to feel ashamed or inadequate? Did your dream-self have any answers to the questions posed by the panel?

THE ISLAND

In the hectic modern world, a desert island represents freedom and escape, a rest from the demands of society. Yet, as Robinson Crusoe discovered, a paradise without exits becomes a nightmarish prison. What emotions were evoked by the island—nostalgic longing or terrifying claustrophobia? How might these feelings relate to situations in your waking life? Are you trapped in a corner from which there seems no escape? A difficult job? An awkward money situation? Was there a hope of rescue in the dream, suggesting possible paths forward?

THE LIBRARY

In dreams, buildings of any description usually signify the dreamer. A library typically represents our intellectual aspect, our place in the world of ideas, and our ability to access knowledge. Consider how you and your fellow readers behaved in your dream library. Did you cause any kind of disturbance to attract other people's attention, or did other readers distract you? Did you have difficulty finding the book you wanted? How might the events in your dream reflect your perception of your intellect? Do you feel your abilities get the respect they deserve?

THE MAP
In our waking lives, the only maps available are those which show us how to get from one physical place to another. The maps in our dreams, while showing mountains and valleys or streets and squares, may help us navigate the more uncertain contours of our careers and relationships. Was your dream map easy to follow? Where did it lead you—into an alien landscape, to a familiar setting, or up a blind alley? Could the map be showing you the way to achieve a goal you have set for yourself, or suggesting a change in direction?

MARRIAGE
Marriage is the cornerstone of the traditional family unit representing security and companionship, a means to share the burden of life's responsibilities. Dreams featuring positive images of marriage may reflect the dreamer's inner stability and confidence in the future. However, if the marriage in your dream is under threat, look for parallels in your own marital relations, or those of parents or friends. Can you identify the cause of the problems in the dream? A breakdown in communication? A cooling of passion?

THE MAZE
The modern world presents us with a bewildering array of choices and decisions. The anxiety that these sometimes provoke can find

expression in dreams in which we are lost in a labyrinth of identical-looking corridors or streets. In your dream, were you alone in the maze? Who or what did you encounter in your wanderings? How might the difficulties of your encounters in the maze reflect a decision that is troubling you in your waking life? How did you manage to find your way out?

THE MIRROR

In our waking lives, we use mirrors to examine ourselves, and so it follows that when they occur in dreams they usually reflect the dreamer's self-image. For example, a strange face in the mirror may indicate an identity crisis, whereas a frightening face may stand for the Shadow, the archetype that represents the dreamer's darker side. Look again into the mirror in your dream and take note of anything that struck you in particular. How might it relate to the way you perceive yourself?

MONEY

Money is a basic token of exchange and is associated not only with material possessions, but with the power, status, and glamour conferred by wealth. Was the quantity of money an issue in your dream? A full purse can denote personal empowerment, acting as a prompt for positive action. However, not having enough money to pay for what you wanted may suggest you feel you lack the skills or qualifications needed to achieve a desired goal. How did your dream-self cope with the shortfall in money?

MUSIC

Composers, from Beethoven to Paul McCartney, have drawn upon harmonies they have dreamed about to influence their work. While we may not always be able to put the music from our dreams to such practical use, it can afford us insights into our personal creativity. Beautiful music can represent the infinite potential of our imagination, whereas the chaos of discordant music may suggest creative potential that has become distorted.

THE PLACE OF WORSHIP

A church or temple can represent the spiritual side of the dreamer, or perhaps a yearning for peace or higher wisdom. A high tower or tall spire would reinforce the image of reaching upward in search of divine inspiration. Did your dream-self feel uncomfortable or unfamiliar in spiritual surroundings? You may be giving too much attention to the material world. Listen to your dream, seek out a quiet place, and, if only for a short while, put worldly worries aside.

THE PUPPET

By their very nature, puppets or marionettes suggest manipulation and a lack of free choice for the person whose strings are being pulled. In your dream, were you the puppet or the puppeteer, or were you a member of the audience? Did the puppet move in the way that the puppeteer intended, or did the strings become entangled? Could your dream be urging you to address an imbalance of power in one of your relationships?

THE RAINBOW

The rainbow is a universal symbol of promise, hope, and redemption. If it appears in your dream, you may be coming toward the resolution of a troubling issue. Alternatively, perhaps the rainbow represents a bridge between this world and your inner life. Are your dreams urging you to connect with your inner sensitivity? Have you been caught up in material or superficial matters and thus been neglectful of your spiritual self?

THE SCHOOL

School experiences are among the most formative in life. They leave a deep imprint on our subconscious and provide a rich vocabulary of dream symbols. School dreams can explore themes as diverse as relationships with figures of authority (usually embodied in the dream as a teacher), yearning for public esteem or approval, and feelings of nostalgia. Is there any issue troubling you in your waking life, which might have given rise to your dream? For example, is someone or something making you feel inadequate? Or, could there be an aspect of your past that you are actively longing for now?

THE SERPENT

Different interpretations of the serpent abound throughout the world, making its meaning difficult to explain in dreams. In the Judeo-Christian tradition, the serpent is seen as a source of evil whose appearance in dreams signifies foreboding. Some cultures view the serpent as a symbol of psychic energy, the intuitive wisdom of the unconscious. In others it heralds healing and new life. Consider your dream response to the serpent. Does this provide a clue to the meaning of the sign?

THE SHADOW

The Shadow is our dark side and our instinctual self. Psychologist Carl Jung names it as one of his archetypes, "the thing that we have no wish to be." The Shadow, impervious to destruction, often appears in nightmares and is usually the same sex as the dreamer, with a threatening presence. Despite its frightening nature, the Shadow is deeply valuable. Its urges may represent a goal that you harbor, and its primal energy will help you conquer obstacles. Search your dream for anything that the Shadow might have been encouraging you to do. How might this represent one of your desires, hidden or otherwise?

THE STAGE

The dream world is itself a theater in which magical transformations occur, images leap from the imagination, and the drama of life unfolds. Some dreams take this metaphor to its natural conclusion, using actual theaters, cinemas, or circuses as their setting. Such dreams may act as a warning not to let appearances mislead you, or they may reflect a desire for more excitement in your life. If your dream-self was one of the performers, what type of role did you play? Did the performance—the plot, the audience reaction, the identities of the actors—have any bearing on issues that are confronting you in your waking life?

TEETH

In dreams, our true feelings about ourselves are often projected through distorted bodily images. Dental problems, such as teeth falling out or breaking, are common in dreams reflecting feelings of insecurity and loss. What do your teeth represent to you? Are you proud of your smile or do you seek to hide it in shame? In the dream, were the teeth wobbly, or did they fall out? What caused this to happen? How can you relate these dental distortions to specific anxieties about your physical appearance? Or perhaps to more general emotional and psychological fears?

TRAVELING

In our stressful society we often find ourselves rushing through the day in the pursuit of necessary material goals. In our dreams, however, we are free to travel as we wish—slowly to fascinating lands or magically through the sky to distant places. If you find yourself embarking upon a dream journey, consider how you traveled: for example, a train ride may convey the sense of following a fixed route, being unable to change direction, or, if you missed your stop, a feeling of missed opportunity.

THE WISE OLD WOMAN

The Wise Old Woman is one of the archetype figures identified by psychologist Carl Jung. A source of instinctive, age-old wisdom, she will appear in your dreams as an older figure—perhaps a parent, a teacher, or a priest. She is the symbol of primal growth and care. Her